LAUGH OUT LOUD WITH LENORE IN THE BOOK OF STUPID QUESTIONS AND ANSWERS

LAUGH OUT LOUD WITH LENORE IN THE BOOK OF STUPID QUESTIONS AND ANSWERS

LENORE DEPP

authorHOUSE®

AuthorHouse™
1663 Liberty Drive
Bloomington, IN 47403
www.authorhouse.com
Phone: 1-800-839-8640

Published by AuthorHouse   08/13/2012

ISBN: 978-1-4772-5566-7 (sc)
ISBN: 978-1-4772-6046-3 (e)

Introduction

The author displays the great sense of humor that God has blessed her with. This book will make you laugh and bring out your wonderful sense of humor. This book will pick you up if you are down. It is a magnet for laughter.

If you enjoy reading something hilarious, this is the book to read and enjoy. This book can be a family activity on a sunny or a rainy day. You can enjoy reading this book to grandparents. It is a very funny book. Please have fun and enjoy reading it.

Stupid Question #1

What would you do if you walked into a dark room with the lights turned out?

    A. Walk into the room and stand on your head.
    B. Walk into the room and look in the mirror.
    C. Walk into the room and jump over the bed.

Stupid Answer:

Stupid Question #2

What would you do if you jumped in your car on your way to work and it would not start?

   A. Sing a song to the car until it started the engine.
   B. Let the hood up and ask what's wrong.
   C. Get out of the car and push it to your destination.

Stupid Answer:

Stupid Question #3

What would you do if you went to buy groceries and discovered that you had no money in your wallet when you got to the checkout register?

A. Ask the clerk if you could borrow some money.
B. Ask the clerk if there is a money tree in the store.
C. Ask the clerk if IOU slips are accepted.

Stupid Answer:

Stupid Question #4

What would you do if your false teeth fell out during a job interview?

    A. Pick them up, put them back in your mouth, and continue talking.

    B. Tell the interviewer that they were not your real teeth anyway.

    C. Ask the interviewer if he knows a good dentist.

Stupid Answer:

Stupid Question #5

What would you do if you were a bank teller and a customer asked to cash his two-dollar check at nine o'clock in the morning?

- A. Tell him the bank is closed.
- B. Tell him the bank had just closed—even if the doors had just opened for business
- C. Take his check, cut it into three pieces, and give it back to him. Tell him that each piece is a dollar—and now he has three dollars.

Stupid Answer:

Stupid Question #6

What would you do if you were a police officer and you arrested someone for public drunkenness?

A. Talk to him like he is your three-year-old son.

B. Spray him with mace until he gives up and confesses that he's not drunk—he's sober.

C. Handcuff him and beat him until he confesses that he's your long-lost dad.

Stupid Answer:

Stupid Question #7

What would you do if you were getting ready for work and noticed a big hole in your sock?

- A. Take the sock off, sew the hole, put the sock back on, and go to work.
- B. Put another sock on over it to cover the hole and go to work.
- C. Take both socks off, put them in your back pocket, and go to work.

Stupid Answer:

Stupid Question #8

What would you do if you woke up with two left feet?

- A. Jump out of bed, run down the street, and scream, "I have two left feet!"
- B. Jump out of bed and put on two left shoes.
- C. Jump out of bed, put your best Sunday shoe on your left foot, and start dancing.

Stupid Answer:

Stupid Question #9

What would you do if you were driving home from the club and accidently ran over your neighbor's dog—and it died?

- A. Jump out of your car and give the dog CPR.
- B. Get out of your car, walk over to the dog, and say, "What's up, dog?"
- C. Park your car in your yard, run over to the neighbor's house, wake him, and tell him that his dog died in your arms after having a massive heart attack.

Stupid Answer:

Stupid Question #10

What would you do if you farted in the car on a first date and it smelled like a rotten egg?

   A. Look over at her with your hand over your mouth and nose and ask if she farted.
   B. Tell her not to light a match because there is a gas smell in the car—and the car might explode.
   C. Look over at her and confess that you did it because your great-grandmother told you that it is better out than in.

Stupid Answer:

Stupid Question #11

What would you do if you could not read or write and a lady at the post office asked you to read a letter from her granddaughter because she could not read or write either?

  A. Pretend that you could not hear the lady.
  B. Tell the lady that you left your best reading glasses at home.
  C. Tell the lady that you will read it and rewrite it for twenty dollars.

Stupid Answer:

Stupid Question #12

If you bumped into an old girlfriend and told her you were a successful lawyer when she asked what you did for a living, what would you do if she stopped at McDonald's and saw you in the back flipping burgers?

A. Pretend that you own the McDonald's.
B. Tell her you are in the uniform because you are investigating a harassment case.
C. Tell her you are not really a lawyer; you're an undercover police officer investigating McDonald's.

Stupid Answer:

Stupid Question #13

What would you do if you were watching TV in your living room and the roof fell in on top of your TV?

  A. Sit there and pretend it was just your imagination.
  B. Think that it was a good floor model TV.
  C. Go to your neighbor's house and ask to borrow his or her TV because the roof fell in on yours.

Stupid Answer:

Stupid Question #14

What would you do if you were hitchhiking and you noticed an alien was driving when a car stopped to give you a ride?

A. Ask the alien if he was on his way to Mars.
B. Ask the alien if he could he beam you up with Scotty.
C. Tell the alien that if he did not take you where you wanted to go, you were going to call immigration to tell them that he was a illegal alien in this country.

Stupid Answer:

Stupid Question #15

What would you do if you were at a family barbeque and your uncle was barbequing a dog on the grill?

    A. Ask your uncle if he got the dog from the pound.

    B. Tell your friends that your uncle is barbequing his new hot dogs—and they need to come get some.

    C. Tell the vet that you found the dog he was looking for—and he is all burnt up.

Stupid Answer:

# Stupid Question #16

What would you do if your fire alarm started buzzing and you saw the kitchen was on fire?

    A. Tell your wife not to worry—she never cooked anyway.

    B. Tell your kids to get against the wall for a fire drill.

    C. Throw a jug of gasoline on the fire to see how big the fire could get.

Stupid Answer:

Stupid Question #17

What would you do if you were walking your dog in the park, and the dog said, "I'm tired. Can we go home now?"

    A. Tell the dog to stop whining.
    B. Ask the dog when he learned how to talk.
    C. Tell the dog to shut up before you dog him out.

Stupid Answer:

Stupid Question #18

What would you do if you were working on your computer and it used a lion's voice to say, "Get out of the office"?

    A. Speak in a cat's meow to tell the computer you won't go.

    B. Slap the computer and tell it to shut up.

    C. Dial 911 and tell the police that your computer threatened you.

Stupid Answer:

Stupid Question #19

What would you do if you inserted your card into the ATM to get $100 and the machine gave you $1,000?

A. Call the police to tell them the ATM gave you too much money.

B. Leave a note on the ATM to let the banker know the machine gave you too much money—and you were sorry for taking it.

C. Call the bank manager after you have spent the money to tell him that you are sorry that the machine gave you too much money—and you will pay them back with an IOU.

Stupid Answer:

Stupid Question #20

What would you do if you had a dream that God put you in hell?

    A. You would have had a cold glass of water before bed.
    B. You would have asked God to loan you a bag of ice before he put you there.
    C. You would have gone to bed naked so that you would be a lot cooler in hell.

Stupid Answer:

Stupid Question #21

If you had a pillow, who would you want to sleep next to you?

A. Someone with good breath so he or she won't gross you out in the morning.
B. Someone with pretty teeth so you would not have to run away if he or she smiled at you.
C. Someone who sleeps with money where his or her mouth is, so that you could rob him or her and leave.

Stupid Answer:

Stupid Question #22

If you were a cellular phone, who would you ring for?

    A. People who are important to themselves.
    B. People who talk to themselves all day.
    C. People who pay their cellular phone bills.

Stupid Answer:

Stupid Question #23

If you were a toilet and you produced money for people who could hit your golden button, what would you do?

    A. Make sure the people who sat on you were rich.

    B. Pray to God that the toilet would only work for your golden behind.

    C. Tell them to sit their broke behind somewhere else.

Stupid Answer:

Stupid Question #24

If you were a set of false teeth and your owner had bad breath, what would you do when your owner put you in his mouth?

    A. Yell for help.
    B. Jump back out with your teeth chattering as if you were sick.
    C. Say, "Man, your breath stinks."

Stupid Answer:

Stupid Answer #25

What would you do if you were a third-grade teacher and one of your students threw his shoe at your head while you were teaching?

- A. Throw the shoe back at his head.
- B. Take your shoe off and throw it at his face.
- C. Throw him out the window with both his shoes off.

Stupid Answer:

Stupid Question #26

What would you do if you caught your wife kissing another man during her lunch break?

A. Smile and ask her if kissing him was part of her job.
B. Ask her if she was playing a kissing game with him.
C. Ask her to kiss you after she kissed him.

Stupid Answer:

Stupid Question #27

What would you do if you found out that your mother and father were kinfolk?

    A. Ask them how close they are so you could document it.
    B. Ask them if they are kissing cousins.
    C. Ask them if it is okay to marry your cousin.

Stupid Answer:

Stupid Question #28

What would you do if you found out that your father was a serial killer?

- A. Ask him what type of cereal he likes for breakfast.
- B. Ask him if he goes by serial numbers before he kills people.
- C. Ask if you could ride around with him at night so you could see what type of serial killer he is.

Stupid Answer:

Stupid Question #29

What would you do if you were pretty white teeth in somebody's mouth and the person had an ugly face?

A. Ask that person to put a bag over his or her face and cut out the teeth part so people could only see your teeth.

B. Put a ski mask on so only your eyes and teeth showed.

C. Pull your teeth out of that person's body and put them up for sale on eBay.

Stupid Answer:

Stupid Question #30

What would you do if you were a pair of Levi's and someone in really bad shape wore you?

    A. Tell that person it's okay to wear you—as long as he or she does not go out in public.

    B. Try to get up and run off the body.

    C. Tell that person to leave you in the closet and to wear Lee jeans instead.

Stupid Answer:

Stupid Question #31

What would you do if the police caught you cooking crystal meth in your kitchen?

 A. Tell the police to put their guns down and have a seat until you are done cooking the crystal meth.
 B. Ask the police if they want to help you finish cooking the crystal meth.
 C. Ask them what took them so long to get there because you were about to go sell it alone.

Stupid Answer:

# Stupid Question #32

What would you do if the book you were reading said, "Why are you reading me?"

  A. Stop reading the book and throw it down.
  B. Ask the book if it is talking to you.
  C. Ask the book to stop complaining.

Stupid Answer:

Stupid Question #33

What would you do if you were a warehouse supervisor and you told an employee to stop clowning around before he got hurt—and he said, "yes, sir" and then slapped you?

- A. Thank him and say, "That was wonderful."
- B. Ask him to do it again.
- C. Say, "Thank you, sir. Now could you please come home with me tonight and slap my wife and my mama because they're getting on my nerves."

Stupid Answer:

Stupid Question #34

What would you do if you worked forty hours and everyone else got their paycheck on payday but the supervisor said, "I'm not going to pay you this week—I will pay you next week"?

- A. Say, "Yes, sir, boss. I will wait until next week."
- B. Tell him that your light bill is due that day.
- C. Say, "Okay, boss. I will just hold you hostage until next payday.

Stupid Answer:

Stupid Question #35

What would you do if your blind date had rotten breath when she was trying to kiss you?

    A. Pretend that you have a cold and cough in her face.

    B. Tell her that you really need to use the bathroom.

    C. Tell her that your mama does not allow you to kiss on the first date.

Stupid Answer:

Stupid Answer #36

What would you do if someone broke into your house while you were cooking and demanded you cook him dinner at gunpoint?

A. Ask why he is in your home while you are cooking dinner.
B. Ask if the gun is loaded.
C. Tell him to put the gun down because dinner is almost ready—and his timing is perfect.

Stupid Question #37

What would you do if your barber accidently cut a big gap in the back of your head—and then laughed about it?

    A. Laugh with him and tell him that's exactly what you wanted.
    B. Ask if he has a barber's license.
    C. Take the clippers from him and cut a big gap in the middle of his head—and then look at each other and laugh.

Stupid Answer:

Stupid Question #38

What would you do if you were jogging in the park and saw two people drop dead while they were jogging?

    A. Continue jogging past them as if nothing had happened.

    B. Stop jogging so they could explain to you how they dropped dead—so that you could explain everything to the police.

    C. Stop jogging and lie down beside them so that you can feel death—and maybe have an out-of-body body experience.

Stupid Answer:

Stupid Question #39

What would you do if you woke up in the middle of the night because you heard two ghosts arguing in your room?

  A. Ask what in the world they are arguing about.
  B. Tell them they need to go to another room because you are trying to sleep.
  C. Tell them you will solve their problem so you can go back to sleep.

Stupid Answer:

Stupid Question #40

What would you do if someone gave you a picture of yourself and it spoke to you?

A. Ask if the picture is talking to you.
B. Talk back to the picture.
C. Show the picture to your friends—and tell them the picture will answer their questions.

Stupid Answer:

Stupid Question #41

What would you do if you were a tissue and someone used you to wipe his or her mouth after dinner—and you knew your purpose was for the bathroom?

    A. Say, "Wow, dude. Your breath really stinks."
    B. Say, "I have never smelled anything else that bad."
    C. Say, "Dude, please use me on the other end because your breath stinks."

Stupid Answer:

Stupid Question #42

What would you do if you were a digital camera and someone was using you to take pictures at a party of really ugly people?

A. Try your best not to flash.
B. Speak to your owner and say, "I'm out of service."
C. Speak to your owner and say, "I'm not a throwaway camera."

Stupid Answer:

Stupid Question #43

What would you do if you were a clock and the person that bought you kept staring at you?

    A. Say, "What are you staring at?"
    B. Shout, "Tick-tock, tick-tock" and hope he will go to sleep.
    C. Say, "Stop staring at me as if I'm a time clock."

Stupid Answer:

Stupid Question #44

What would you do if you were a toenail clipper and someone with ugly feet and toes was using you to clip his ugly toenails?

A. Tell him today is your off day.
B. Tell him you were designed just for pretty toenails.
C. Tell him you will call the cops if he cuts his ugly toenails with you.

Stupid Answer:

Stupid Question #45

What would you do if you were a recordable CD and someone with a terrible voice was using you to record a song?

A. Tell them you are a DVD recordable device and can't be used that way.
B. Tell him you are a professional CD—and you don't do unprofessional singers.
C. Fall off the desk so that he can't use you because you would rather be broken than have his voice break you.

Stupid Answer:

Stupid Question #46

What would you do if you were a pair of shoes and someone with stinky feet wanted to buy you?

A. Pretend that you were another brand that he did not like.
B. Tell him you are only on display and not for sale.
C. Run out the shoe store screaming, "Help me! He's trying to put me on his feet."

Stupid Answer:

Stupid Question #47

What would you do if you were a can of air freshener and someone only used you to freshen up a room that was already fresh—and the neighbor wanted to use you for his bathroom after he had a bowel movement?

    A. Make sure when he went to spray you that you did not work
    B. Tell him you were not made for that kind of stinky environment.
    C. Tell him you want to go back home to your mama because her house is fresh.

Stupid Answer:

Stupid Question #48

What would you do if you were a self-help book that promoted positive words and positive people—and a negative person bought you and spoke bad words around you?

A. Say, "Hey, dude. I'm positive and your negative—we don't mix."
B. Pray to God that he goes blind right before reading you.
C. Tell him that you will pay him to sell you to a positive person.

Stupid Answer:

Stupid Question #49

What would you do if you were water release pills and a fat person claimed you did not work?

A. Tell that person you were designed for people with excess water in their bodies—not for people who are naturally fat.
B. Tell that person you only work for people who like you.
C. Tell that person you are steroids—and that is why they keep gaining weight.

Stupid Answer:

Stupid Question #50

What would you do if you were a Rolls-Royce and a low-class drug dealer bought you—and you knew he would cramp your style?

A. Say, "Look, man. I'm a Ford Escort—and you don't want to buy me."
B. When he got in the car and cranked you up, you took over and drove to the police department to give him a hint.
C. You told him you are were made for pimping—you were made to make people with class look good.

Stupid Answer:

About the Author

In this book, Lenore Depp goes deep into the hilarious mindset that God has given her. She wrote this book to read and enjoy with friends and family. This book reflects how she lives her life—having fun, being positive, and not letting anything upset her or kill her joy.

Life is too short to live without laughing. Be filled with a great sense of humor. Every reader will enjoy this book—it will bring laughter to your day. The author wrote *Stupid Questions and Stupid Answers* for her children to enjoy. Readers will gain a great sense of humor. God Bless—and stay hilarious.

CPSIA information can be obtained
at www.ICGtesting.com
Printed in the USA
LVHW090941241021
701372LV00003B/106

9 781477 255667